Letting Go Of Baby

A story of never-ending faith after the heartbreak of miscarriage
By Tamar Knibye

Letting Go Of Baby
Printed by CreateSpace, An Amazon.com Company
Copyright © 2014

Acknowledgements

Thank you to everyone who showed me support during this time in my life. Those who stopped by just to bring me something special, a favorite snack, a game to play, dinner; you will never know how much it meant to me. You did not try to say a clever phrase to make me feel better and give advice on this, that, or the other. Your actions spoke louder than any word that could have been said. Just those acts of kindness helped me day after day.

Thank you to the awesome women who allowed me to include their stories in the book. I know that it brought back memories and feelings. I know that from reliving what you went through someone else will be able to make it through. Nikki, Lajuana, Donna, Rashieda, and Monica; your stories continue to inspire me and I have no doubt they will bring hope and strength to others.

Thank you to my husband who wanted nothing more than to take on the pain himself so I would not have to bear it. You made sure I had me time, rest time, just time to heal. Thank you for being there.

Thank You God for never leaving me nor forsaking me. Thank you for your healing. You were there at the beginning of it all and at the end. I know it was only You who gave me the strength to support others during my time of grief. You have a purpose for everything and I would not be where I am without You!

Table Of Contents

Foreword

Who would have thought that December 1, 2008 would change the rest of my life. Hello, my name is Tamar Knibye and this is my story of letting go of my baby.

I wanted to write this book to encourage women who have had a miscarriage, multiple miscarriages, an ectopic pregnancy, and/or have experienced a stillborn birth. Life is not over when tragedy occurs. As women, we are resilient. We have the inherent ability to endure, and get through hard times of loss. However, no one is an island. Though we may be resilient, there are times that encouragement, prayer, and assistance is necessary. Therefore, this book is to let you know that you are not alone. You do not have to go through this alone. Time will heal, and as you read I pray that you will begin to experience a mending of your heart and life even as I have.

Introduction

I was your average child. I grew up with four siblings. I was the firstborn of my parents and there were three under me. There was my cousin, whom my parents had guardianship over, who was like my older sister. Then there was my sister (we are only 11 months apart so we were like twins most of our lives), my younger brother separated by two and a half years and then there was my youngest brother whom we adopted when I was nine years old. I lived in the suburbs of Alabama. I went to public school where the classrooms were only separated by dividers rather than walls. As school aged children we all had our dreams of what we were going to be when we grew up. I always knew since I was four years old that I would be teacher. Later it was narrowed down to a math teacher and even further to a kindergarten teacher.

At 12 years old my family and I moved to Delaware. The north was the complete opposite of the slow pace of Alabama. At first we missed home quite a bit. However, as teens my siblings and I all agreed that there was more to do in and around Delaware than in our hometown in Alabama. So I did what most teens did. I experienced a crush here and there. I went to a homecoming dance, and proms, and there were even some heart breaks. I took honors classes in high school, but engaged in minimal afterschool activities. I had a few close friends and I was not what you considered a popular girl in school. I was always in the background, but because of my personality type I did not mind it at all.

Among friends, family, and neighbors, I became the go to babysitter. I came to be viewed as the teen that most enjoyed working with kids. Even as a teen, deep in my heart there was a strong desire to someday be married and have children of my own.

As I went on to college my dreams of being a teacher drew closer and closer. I also started participating more in extracurricular activities joining various clubs (e.g. S.O.A.R., schools step team). I enjoyed college a lot. It actually helped me come out of my shell and to become who I am today. I met my life long friends there and even though now we are hundreds of miles away we can still pick up where we left off whenever we call. I graduated cum laude and went on to become a kindergarten teacher.

Teaching was great! I was single, had my ideal job but longed for the next phase in my life to begin. But then it snuck up on me. A tall young man began to attend my church. Every other Sunday he would come to help out by playing the drums. His name was Tsombawi Knibye, Jr. He saw me and pursued me. However, he did not begin his pursuit until after he had spoken to my dad to ask if he could even date me. Because of his old fashioned and honorable approach, it was a big plus in the eyes of my parents, as well as my own. Yes, he and I did get married. On July 21, 2007 we had the most beautiful ceremony with all of our friends and family, with weather perfectly designed by God. Loving children as much as I did, I looked forward to becoming a mother. However, my husband and I agreed to wait about a year before trying to start a family. This is where our true journey began.

Chapter 1

Life has come!
*"... and God hearkened to her, and opened her **womb**." (Genesis 30:22)*

It was Friday, September 12, 2008 when I followed my suspicions and took a pregnancy test, and just as I had suspected the test was positive. This was quite interesting due to the fact that all week different people were alluding to the fact that they thought I was pregnant (the school secretary, one of my student's parents, and my husband). We had to go to a banquet at church that night and I started to feel the first of the symptoms on the way there. It was hard not to tell anyone, including my in-laws who were also at the banquet. We wanted to get the blood test to be completely sure before we told anyone. The funny thing was I appeared really bloated and I already looked like I was a couple of months pregnant even though I was a couple of weeks. Fortunately for us no one noticed, and because of the cold, I kept my coat on almost the entire night.

Monday, September 15th, I was on my way to get blood work at Lab Corp when my younger sister called me out of the blue. She just happened to ask me if I was pregnant yet. As I told her the news of the pregnancy test, all I heard was screaming and crying in the background. She said she was outside at the time and she had to go inside the house because she was screaming so loud. She was so excited that she could not contain herself. I, myself, felt proud at my younger sister's response.

Since I worked in a small school with around 275-300 K-3rd grade students, it was easy for news to get around quickly. On Tuesday morning, before school started, one person in the office found out and from there, it spread through the school like wildfire. It went up and down the hallways like a runaway dog! People were coming to my classroom saying "there's going to be a little Knibye soon." I was happy, they were happy and we were all excited.

We still had not told our parents yet because the blood work had not come back but we wanted it to be special when we did tell them. The test came back positive so we planned to tell his parents on Sunday. Tsombawi (my husband) decided to make his parents an original card telling them that they were going to be grandparents and his brother that he was going to be an uncle. Again, they were happy and excited and so were we. I decided to buy both my parents and wrote a little note in them.

My dad opened his card and just looked at me. Then looked at the card and looked at me again and started smiling and laughing. He was so excited. My dad showed my brother his card. My brother looked at me and replied with "Tamar you pregnant!" He decided immediately that it was going to be a girl. My mother was in Alabama with her mother at the time, so she would not be getting her card for another day until she returned.

Wednesday I got an email from my mother telling me congratulations and how proud of me she was. She had just returned home from a trip and she read my card at 1:00 am in the morning. She said she screamed when she read it. I felt really special that she would send me an email like that. She asked if she could send out a mass email letting family and friends know the news. So the word was out. My family knew, my husband's family knew. Everything was going great. I started showing very early. There was speculation from friends that there might be more than one in there but I was just happy to be carrying a baby.

On November 5, 2008, I was 3 months pregnant and we heard the heartbeat of the baby. It was unbelievable, 171 nice and strong. The doctor found a heartbeat right away. There was really something in their growing in my belly. My kindergarten students knew that I was pregnant and would constantly ask about when the baby was coming. A few students from the year before also knew and asked questions too. I had one student tell me that she would say "Congratulations" every time she saw me; and she did. My best friend wanted to know how I looked so I took a picture and sent it to her on November 15, 2008.

 Things were going great. We had no worries and there was absolutely no reason to worry anyway. My family was going to be here on Thanksgiving and we were going to have a good time. My sister and her husband came up from North Carolina. They had not seen me since the news of my pregnancy. My sister gave me a new hair-do and she and my mom even bought me some new cute outfits that I could expand in. We all went bowling together but I did not bowl because I did not want to over strain my body, due to my

pregnancy. Thanksgiving came and went and so did Friday, Saturday, and Sunday. Still, there was nothing out of the ordinary.

Monday morning came. It was December 1, 2008 and it was time to go back to school after Thanksgiving break. I was getting dressed when all of the sudden I felt this sharp pain in my shoulder. I would have endured the pain except it went down my side and went to a cramping in my belly. I called my mom and then I called the doctor. She told me that it might be indigestion. So I took some Tums and drank some water, then waited an hour. By that time my mom had come to my house and we were waiting to see if the pain would go away. The pain did not reside so the doctor instructed me to go to triage (OB emergency room).

When I arrived, around 10:15am, I filled out the paperwork and went to the first room. The lady asked me a few questions about the pain and then as a precaution looked for the heartbeat of the baby. She could not find it but there were no concerns. Her response was that my uterus might be tilted. The doctors would try again in the back room. So I went to the room and got in the bed. One doctor came in and gave me Tylenol for the pain and tried to take blood. For some odd reason, she could not find my vain. The nurses tried three times but failed. This had never happened before when giving blood and they caused me pain from poking me so much. Nevertheless, I still felt normal other than the strange shoulder pain.

Another doctor came in and tried to assess my condition. Maybe it was just a muscle spasm or something minor. As a precaution he tried again to check the heartbeat of the baby to make sure it was fine. At that point he still could not find the heartbeat. So he said when they could not find the heartbeat they would do an ultrasound. So I was transported downstairs for x-rays to see if anything was causing the pain and to check the baby's heartbeat.

The x-ray was fast and simple. It took forever for the hospital to transport me to the ultrasound room. Once in, the technician began the ultrasound right away. I had never had an ultrasound before so I thought that the silence was the way it was supposed to occur. She took many pictures but never looked at me or said a word. I had no idea what I was looking at on the screen. It was not facing me directly so I could not see much anyway. She did this for about 10 minutes in complete silence, just the sound of a clicking mouse. When finished, she said she would show the doctor the results. She went and got the doctor; he came in looked at the pictures and walked right out. He never even looked at me or said a thing. The technician said I would be transported back upstairs and the doctor would give me the results.

After the x-rays, ultrasounds, monitors, and attempted blood work the time was around 2:00pm. Back in the room, my husband finally arrived after work around 2:10pm. My mom left the room since my husband was there and went to visit my pregnant friend on the second floor. About 5 minutes later the doctor and nurse came in. The news came something like this . . .

"Well, the tests came back fine, but unfortunately the baby has died."

It was very unemotional almost like it was the norm. He proceeded to tell me that I was 17 weeks and the baby only dated 14 weeks and 2 days. So the baby had stopped breathing probably a week prior to that day. There was no explanation why only that sometimes these things happen. Sitting there as he talked about different things was very surreal (It was all a blur). I could not believe what I was hearing. My heart just dropped. This was not real;

16

he did not just tell me that my baby died. I could not move, or speak. It was not until he started going over options to remove the baby that I started to cry. The options were to be induced to go into labor and deliver, have a D & E procedure, or just wait until the baby came out on its own (which could take weeks). They said they would give us a minute to make a decision and left the room. I just started crying. I called my mom right away. All I could get out was the word "*mom*" through a crying voice and she said she would be right down. As soon as she came in we told her what the doctor said as I cried and cried and cried. The one thing that stuck in my head that she said when I was crying was "*God knows best.*" I believed that with all my heart, and I never asked why me, why this but nevertheless, the pain was still there. It was the longest day of my life.

For the next 4 days every time I looked at my belly I cried because the baby was still there but it was no longer living. We decided on getting the D & E procedure. We thought they would schedule it the next day but they made me wait for the rest of the week. Thank God for my husband because they were going to make me wait until the following week to have the baby removed but he stressed that I could not go any longer with a non-living baby in my womb.

It was enough to have the baby die but to have to walk around with it was the hard part.

December 5th, 2008 was the day of the procedure. I never knew whether the baby was a boy or girl. The procedure itself was already so gruesome for a baby that I did not want to go through the process of waiting for tissue to be sent off and return with results weeks later. If they could not tell me right after the procedure then I did not want to know. I had to move on and continue with faith and hope that we would hold our new baby one day.

It was hard initially because students would make reference to having the baby yet. Not to mention there were pregnant people all around me. Two co-workers at school, my co-worker from the tutoring center, my friend from church, my husband's college friend and yes, my sister. She told me she was pregnant the same month I found out my baby died. I was constantly confronted with new moms having healthy babies. Even the moms of three of my students were pregnant.

I had no choice but to try to not think about my hurt and be happy for those around me. I really had to put my trust in God to heal my heart. There

18

was too much new life happening for me to wallow in my sorrow. I started doing things on purpose like going to visit those who just had their baby. Exactly a week after I found out about my loss, I went to see my friend who had just delivered. It was a very bittersweet moment but I knew I had to go and support her. I went to baby showers; I bought baby gifts. I wanted to go all out for each person. It was not all about me, God had a plan and I was willing to go with the plan. Just keeping in mind that my day would come.

Chapter 2

Could it Be?

"Hope deferred makes the heart sick, but when the desire comes, it is a tree of life" (Proverbs 13:12 NKJV)

We waited after my first menstrual cycle following my procedure before we started trying again. I wanted it to happen right away. I wanted to be pregnant again so the void would be gone. People were waiting for me to get pregnant. The constant questioning added more pressure and the need to fill the void was hanging over my head. I was still letting God heal me but I also still wanted a baby right away. To my surprise my first cycle came the second week in January. Yes, that did seem fast but it came and we were ready to try again.

On Sunday, February 8, 2009, another positive test told me I was pregnant again. At first it was very faint but then it came in very clear. I had a familiar feeling earlier that day. I was really uncomfortable in my clothes. I told my husband I thought I was pregnant so he said take the test. So there I was pregnant again. Of course I was excited. It had happened so fast. My cycle was late by only one day by that time. So, I decided to wait to go to the doctor or call about blood work. But once Monday arrived I felt like I needed to go ahead and call in for blood work.

When I went to get the blood work, I decided to buy a dollar store pregnancy test just to take it again. I had used one for my first pregnancy and it was quite accurate. I took the test when I got back to school but it was extremely faint, not like the first one I took the day before. It never did come in completely clear. At this moment I was just trying to push away any negative thoughts from my head. This was our second pregnancy and surely we were going to have a successful one. Only positive thoughts were allowed. My co-worker had found out that day too. She just happened to ask me after school if my husband and I were going to try again. I kept silent and just looked at her. She put two and two together with going to get blood work that afternoon; she knew I was pregnant again. Of course she was happy for me. The paraprofessional working in my room walked in while she was hugging me and so she knew too. I was just a little uneasy because I did not want anyone to know yet. I was just going to wait for the belly to pop out and then the news would be out.

Wednesday, February 11ᵗʰ came and I got the call from the nurse. My HCG numbers were low (around 64) but I was still very early in the pregnancy so she sent me to get more blood work that day just to make sure my numbers went up like they are supposed to. That night when I went home, I was extremely tired and nauseated and just fell asleep on the couch. These were familiar symptoms that I recognized from the first pregnancy. Surely, because the symptoms started everything was all right. Two days went by and I waited on Friday for the nurse to call me and tell that my numbers were doing what they are supposed to do. I did not wait for her to call me because that day I had cramping and spotting while I was at work, so I called her.

While I was on the phone doing a parent conference the nurse called me on my cell phone. I could not wait to get a message so I told the parent to hold on. I answered the phone and the nurse said my numbers only went up by 5 and my progesterone went down. My HCG levels were supposed to double in two days; and since I was spotting she said I might be miscarrying. I did not want to believe it. My heart dropped. But I could not get upset because I still had a parent on the other phone. The nurse ordered another blood test for Monday to see what my numbers would do.

22

All kinds of things went through my mind. Maybe it was implantation bleeding but if it was it would have happened weeks ago. Women have bled during pregnancy and still went full term. Maybe we should have waited longer to try. What was happening here? By Saturday, February 14, Valentine's Day, the bleeding had picked up and the cramping was worse. I could hardly walk around the house because of the cramping. I lay on the bed in tears because I did not want to lose another baby. I did not think that I could handle something else like that again and so soon. My husband did the only thing he knew to do. He just left it to God. He put on some encouraging music to build my faith and left to do the errands that I was going to do. He returned to a calmer wife and brought me a dozen roses. That made my day. For the rest of the day I stayed on the couch. We could not even attend the Valentine's banquet because I could not move around.

As the weekend continued I waited patiently for Monday to arrive for the next round of blood work. I was originally planning to go to New York to get baby furniture from my best friend. She had promised it to me during my first pregnancy and said that I could still have it. It was President's Day so I did not have to worry about going to work. Sunday came and went and I was still cramping and bleeding too much to walk around.

Finally it was Monday and I slowly got myself together to go to Lap Corp for more blood work. I was pretty sure they knew my face by now since I had been there quite a few times in the past two weeks. My body felt so bad that after I left Lab Corp, I called the doctor to see if I could get an appointment that day. She called back and said she would have to schedule me for Wednesday and order more blood work too.

Wednesday arrived and I had to leave school early to make my appointment. The two people that knew why I was going were rooting for me to have some good news to share. I went to the doctor for my appointment. They did blood work right away. Now it was time to face the doctor. She asked me the usual questions to try to give a diagnosis of why I was cramping, bleeding, numbers were increasing, but they were still low. Her two assumptions were either I was having a miscarriage or it was ectopic. She sent me to the ultrasound room.

This ultrasound was a much better experience. There was a screen that I myself could look at. The technician was really nice and she explained everything that I was looking at from my uterus to the fallopian tubes. I, of course, still did not know what to look for to determine if I was having a miscarriage or if it was ectopic but she did. Before she began she did express that if it was an ectopic pregnancy that we might not see anything because I was still early in the pregnancy. When she finished the process she called my doctor in. The first thing she said to her while looking at the pictures was "I do not think she is missing". Then they looked at the pictures some more and had a very surprised looked on their face. They were looking at a white dot on the screen and looking at the measurements of it.

The diagnosis was made. I had an ectopic pregnancy. The egg had moved into my ovaries. The interesting thing about that is that it is very rare for the egg to go anywhere but the fallopian tubes. When it is in the fallopian tubes you might not be able to see it until weeks later and by that time you might be experiencing great pain and have to go to surgery to get the zygote removed. That in turn would cause you to lose part of your fallopian tube. But again, God was watching over me. Because the zygote was in my ovaries, it was spotted early. She told me this time that I needed to wait until my numbers were negative again and then wait two full cycles before trying to get pregnant again. That would set me back another two months (or so I thought). My doctor sent me right to triage so that I could get the medicine (methotrexate) which would cause the zygote to dissolve back into my body.

By the time I reached triage my husband had arrived. The scene was all too familiar, the room, the needles, and the circumstances. When the doctor was taking some more blood the tears started to flow again. As she left the room I uttered the words "I can't do this anymore." All my husband could do was let me fall asleep crying. I knew I was spared from losing part of my reproductive organs but there was still that feeling of loss and hurt. I had lost baby number two. When would my turn come? The wait was going to be longer.

After the process was completed, I was free to go home. The doctor had told us that it might take 1 to 3 months for everything to be back to normal. My numbers were already low so he had a good prognosis for me. When we went home I decided to do some extra research on ectopic pregnancies to see what exactly I was saved from.

The thing that stood out to me that changed my whole perspective was the fact that one site said it was *"the number one cause of first trimester maternal death."* Words could not express how relived I felt. God had not only protected my ability to reproduce, but He saved me from death. Right then I knew that I was in His hands and that I now understood that His timing is His timing and He knew what was best for me. I could not feel sorry for myself because some women go through the other side of ectopic pregnancies such as emergency surgeries, damaged reproductive organs, or death.

That whole process took me from February to April just to get my numbers back to zero. Then I had to wait from April to May to have two full cycles. It had been six months since I lost the first baby. May was supposed to be my due date for the first baby. Yes, the thoughts of I would have had a baby by now came across my head but I did not dwell on it. The key was not to dwell and pity myself. I wanted to be strong for others because some women needed therapy just to get through things like this. I had everything I needed, God, my family, and hope to make it through. I refused to feel defeated and be defeated. My time would come and when it did I was going to let others know that they can make it too.

Chapter 3

The Wait

"I would have lost heart, unless I had believed that I would see the goodness of the LORD In the land of the living." (Psalm 27:13 NKJV)

When things like this happen, the wait makes it that more stressful. Every couple of days before my next cycle my mind would be consumed with questions of was I pregnant or was it just symptoms of PMS. All day I would think about it. Not that I was sitting around purposefully thinking about it but the thoughts would pop in my head. Then, if I thought I was pregnant, other concerns would come into my head. Things like what if it's ectopic again. That would only make the wait months away again because of recovery time. To top it off, there are the people who are waiting for me to be pregnant again. Like before, students and adults alike were asking if I was pregnant again or was I going to try soon. Most of them did not know about the ectopic so, for them, I was just waiting a long time.

In the month of June alone I probably took about 3 or 4 pregnancy tests. I was not rushing it, then again maybe I was, but I did not want to be doing something that would hurt the baby if I were

28

pregnant and did not know it. I was so convinced that I was pregnant in June because I was extremely bloated and I had a little nausea too. I just kept saying oh I know I am I remember this feeling. Well . . . June came and went with a cycle. I was not pregnant, yet.

Then July came. I told myself that I was not going to test until the day or days after my cycle had come. Those few days before the date were like eternity. Four days late and I took the pregnancy test. I waited for the 3 minutes to pass while I anticipated the results. "Not Pregnant" came across the screen. In my mind I wondered how could that be. I felt myself beginning to well up inside. But I could not dwell on that moment. I still had stuff to do that day and I believed what Psalm 27 said, *"I would have lost heart, unless I had believed that I would see the goodness of the LORD In the land of the living".* I was now seven days late so I decided to take the test again. It still read negative. But for some reason I was not convinced that the test was right. I even had a little spotting the next morning. By Tuesday, the bleeding and cramps had begun. Now I had started looking really bloated which is not out of the ordinary for me but when my cycle begins it usually goes away right away. I stayed bloated. Even my husband noticed it. I wanted to make sure that nothing else was going on since there was that prior ectopic pregnancy. So, the doctor sent me for blood work (She said for my peace of mind).

Thursday, I got the call at work. She said the blood test came back negative. I had already made up in my mind that no matter what she told me I still had this feeling. That feeling stayed with me for the next month. Everyday it was on my mind. When I would try to not think about it I would look in the mirror and see that I still looked bloated. Then I had a low level of nausea everyday. I had to constantly pray for peace in my mind because I would think about it all day, everyday.

August came and the birth of my niece was the new news on the block. It was almost unreal that my younger sister had given birth to a baby girl. I decided to go and show my excitement and support for her so I surprised her by flying in 3 days after she gave birth. She was excited to see me and I was excited to see her and the baby. I was only there three days but one of those days became very hard for me. No one knew or could even tell that I was crying internally. My heart still ached a little bit. I fought thoughts; negative thoughts against my sister, self-pity thoughts. It hurt when she was giving me tips to hold the baby and pregnancy tips. In my head I was thinking, "Yeah, I already know some of this remember I was pregnant too." At that point she still had no knowledge of my second pregnancy and I didn't want to put a damper on the occasion. I prayed, pleaded with God that He would take away this self-pity feeling I had going on. This was not about me and it was not my sister's fault. God had set this time for her to give birth and be a mother and my goal was to rejoice in this time and help her wherever I could.

I thank God that He answered my prayer. On the last day I was there I felt like I helped even more than the first two days without reservation or grudgingly. I was happy for them. I had a niece and she was just beautiful. I loved her and my sister.

Meanwhile, I let go of tracking my ovulation days. I figured that when God was ready for me to get pregnant then that was when I would get pregnant. School was starting again as well as my cycle. It was due to start around the 18th of August. I figured I would take it easy with unpacking boxes and everything, you know, just to be on the safe side. One day, two days . . . eight days late again. Since this was a similar situation from the last month I told myself that I would not jump the gun

31

to take another test. Besides, God had told me to wait (keyword here) and take the test on Friday. Friday would have been about 11 days past due my cycle.

So I waited until early Friday morning. As soon as I woke up I knew I would not be able to go back to sleep until I took the test. So I did. The first line that came up was the pregnant line. Results: YOU'RE PREGNANT! It was like I was in a dream because I had dreamed about being pregnant before. Then I would wake up and reality would hit. Well, this was reality and I was pregnant. I wanted to make it my goal not to compare this one to the other two pregnancies. I did not want to get discouraged and be worried or stressed out. I did have an emotional scare two days after I found out I was pregnant.

I woke up on a Sunday morning and did not feel as sick as I had the night before. It looked like my stomach went down (mind you I was only five weeks at the time so I was not really showing anyway). My mind was playing tricks on me. When I laid down something said "there is something wrong, you lost it. It happened again." Right then I had to pull down every thought and bring it under subjection (*2 Corinthians 10:5 KJV*). There was nothing wrong at all . I just thanked God for giving me peace in my mind. I knew that those thoughts would try to come here and there but I had to ignore and reject them and only think and say positive things.

My first appointment was scheduled for September 14th. This was just a routine prenatal counseling session that happens for all patients. An unexpected phone call from my doctor turned it into more. They wanted me to get an ultrasound; you know just to be on the safe side. I was relieved that they wanted to take the precaution but of course, all those thoughts came rolling into my head. I only spoke good things. I trusted God and I was not going to let my faith waiver. The ultrasound went great. The heartbeat was strong, although we could not hear it, and the baby was exactly where it should have been in utero. What shocked the doctor was that the baby was conceived on the same side that I had the ectopic. She herself was happy to see that the tube was fine and that everything was going great. All I could think of was that it was only because of God. It was nothing that the medicine or the doctors did.

Chapter 4

The Wait is Over

"But let him ask in faith, with no doubting, for he who doubts is like a wave of the sea driven and tossed by the wind. For let not that man suppose that he will receive anything from the Lord;"(James 1:6-7 NKJV)

My next appointment was October 9th when I would actually hear the heartbeat for the first time. I knew every thing was all right. I trusted God but for some reason I was still worrying. Worry and trust definitely do not mix. It was hard to sleep and to stay in peace the days leading up to the appointment. But then I read James 1: 6-7

"But let him ask in faith, with no doubting, for he who doubts is like a wave of the sea driven and tossed by the wind. For let not that man suppose that he will receive anything from the Lord;"

God gave me the supernatural strength to think positive. Of course, as I went in the doctor had to run down all of what had happened in the past. She was a different doctor than the one whom I had before so I was already starting fresh. She made sure to remind me that this was a different pregnancy, which was going to be a success. The doctor knew I was waiting to hear the heartbeat so she did that first. In the beginning she could only hear my heart beating. It was so loud that she had a hard time finding the baby's heartbeat but she did. The number was 171. I remember the number easily because it was the same number the baby from the first pregnancy had. But this was a different pregnancy and God was holding the baby and me in His arms. The weeks before my next appointments were a journey but I just continued to confess God's word, speak positive things, and pray over the baby and I.

Tuesday, December 1, 2009 came. This was a very pivotal day because we were going to find out the sex of the baby. It was exactly a year, December 1, 2008 when I received the saddening news of the first baby. This was a new year, new doctor, new baby, and new mindset. I took off the entire afternoon from work because I wanted this to be a special day, plus the ultrasound that was scheduled would be 2 hours long. The first part of the appointment involved a counseling session of the family history. The second part was the ultrasound. Watching that little ticker on the screen pumping away was a wonderful feeling. The next thing she said was "this sticking out was the umbilical cord and this sticking out is not, IT'S A BOY." The rest of the ultrasound was all routine checks. Now that we knew it was a boy we could refer to him by name. He would be named after his father. His name would be Tsombawi, meaning *man of peace*. Tsombawi was very cooperative during the session; she got some good shots of him. It was finally time to make the announcement. Mainly co-workers, church members, and immediate family already knew that I was pregnant. Now it was time to let others know and tell everyone it was a boy. Throughout the next weeks and months, I never stopped praying. Even after the doctors had to get an EKG on the baby and told me my blood flow was abnormal, I still trusted God. My pregnancy continued to do well and I was quickly approaching my April 27th due date.

Monday, March 29th was any ordinary day of school and work. I was not feeling any more or less tired. I was working late at school. It was the week before Spring break and I did not know what to expect that next week. My plan was to try not to nest while I was at home. But I wanted to be prepared for my upcoming maternity leave. Everything had to be organized and ready for the new teacher. It had to have been around 6:00 that night and who walks in the room? It was none other than my husband. He had surprised me by coming to the school but to my surprise he did not just come to see me. My co-worker and students had organized a surprise baby shower. He was there to celebrate with me. I was so touched by the thoughtfulness of those around me to want to do something like that on my behalf. This was actually my second baby shower. I had one at the end of February with my friends and family. To get to that point, in and of itself, was amazing for me. I was so close to the promise but even closer than what I had realized. So we left from the school to take party food to share it with my family. I had not realized how my body changed over the past few weeks. My dad made mention of my belly being so low it looked like the baby would be coming soon. But of course not because this was March 29th and I was not due until April 27th.

Well God of course had other plans because a little after 1:00 am my water broke and off to the hospital we went. The labor and delivery was nothing like what you see on TV with all the drama and screaming and yelling and just craziness. Now an epidural did help with keeping the situation nice and calm but even the delivery was calm. Waiting in a quiet room for the next contraction to push and low and behold we welcomed Tsombawi Knibye III into this world at 6:34 pm on Tuesday, March 30, 2010. He was 4 weeks early but healthy nonetheless.

We enjoyed our time with our son. He was the first grand boy on my side of my family and the first grandbaby in the family on my husband's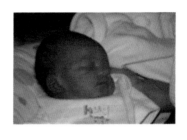
side. Picture taking all the time and videoing every first step, first bite of food, and first words became part of our lives. But the blessing was not over. Just before Tsombawi's first birthday I attended a bridal shower. While there a friend of mine took a good look at me and insisted that I needed to "check" (Of course I knew what she meant). Granted I had been bloated and most women bloat around their cycle. Well I was still bloated and my cycle was late. Too curious to wait until I got home, I ran out on my break at work to get a pregnancy test from the dollar store. There was that double pink line again. I could not believe it. It was sooner than we planned. How could I be pregnant again already? We had been aiming for at least 2 years apart but that was obviously not going to be the case. Tsombawi was not even out of diapers or walking yet.

Nonetheless, we were excited about our new addition to the family. I was being honored that June so my mom and sister decided to buy me a new outfit. My sister was in town for Tsombawi's first birthday party and we were out shopping. Because of my small shape they wanted to pick out a size 1 but I told them that might not fit by then. They stopped and looked at each and then stared at me. They asked if I was pregnant and the answer was yes. And I think this time instead of being excited they were stunned. The news was finally out. What made it even more exciting was the fact that we found out it was a girl. A boy and a girl, "A rich man's family". The pregnancy itself went well. However, I did have to go to triage yet again before the birth. In August 2011, I was getting my class ready for the school year and I sat in a chair and the metal legs broke right from under the chair and down I went. I thank God because he was truly watching over the baby. I spent hours at the hospital but everything turned out perfectly fine.

Baby number two was already showing a different personality. She wanted to come out when she was ready. We all assumed she would come early since Tsombawi was early. Baby girl went all the way to the day before the due date. The doctors decided to induce me because they mentioned something about the placenta (I can never remember the technical terms) and they wanted to be on the safe side. On Tuesday November 15, 2011 we were blessed with a baby girl, Kadesh Tamara Knibye! Less than 2 years from the birth of our son.

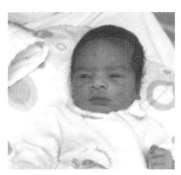

There I was, now a mother of two amidst the pain that we had went through almost 3 years ago. I thank God for these little blessings so much. "*Lo, children are an heritage of the Lord: and the fruit of the womb is his reward*" *(KJV Psalm 127:3)*. They have purpose in this world because they are here and I want to help them find their purpose. I thank God for entrusting his precious children to me for the time they are here on this earth. No one purposefully wants to feel pain and heartache but I would not change it if that is what it took to get these two into the world.

I have found that when you let go of trying to make things happen on your own, God will move in and make things happen the way it should. I had to learn that, <u>You should not try to rush God</u>. I have also discovered that "Letting go of baby" is not completely possible. You never forget the one or ones you lose. They stay with you always. Never let them go because someone else might need to know your story, even your own children.

God allows things to happen in our lives whether they are good or bad for a reason. If everything we experienced was positive how would we know the true goodness of God. You learn to appreciate what you have by those things you lost. I always wonder if I had not lost the two children, would I still have Tsombawi and Kadesh right now? My job was not to continue to wonder, "If I try again, will I lose a third one?" If I did that then they would not exist right now. Trusting and believing is what must be done. I urge you to keep moving forward and continue to live life knowing that your day for motherhood WILL COME one way or another.

"And we know that all things work together for good to them that love God, " (Romans 8:28)

"Trust in the Lord with all thine heart; and lean not unto thine own understanding. In all thy ways acknowledge him, and he shall direct thy paths."(KJV Proverbs 5-6)

41

You Are Not Alone

Read stories from other women who have lost a child/children but did not lose hope and have gone on to become mothers regardless of their obstacles. "They overcame by the blood of the lamb, and by the word of their testimony." (*Revelations 12:11*).

Kimberley's story

In 1994 at the age of 18 I experienced my first miscarriage. It was a traumatizing experience for me at such a young age. I felt so alone inside, but I had the support and comfort of my family to help me get through. It took a lot out of me mentally and physically, but I managed to make it through.

In 1998 I had my second miscarriage. This was also a very hard time for me because I was in the process of planning my wedding so that was a very stressful time as well.

I feel that both of my miscarriages happened for a reason. I believe God allowed this to happen because if I were to carry these babies full term there may have been birth defects or something wrong with the baby to not allow it to live. Or maybe even He (God) felt like it wasn't my time to be a mother. As a woman you want to give up because you feel like it is your job to be able to carry and to give that miracle of life to your husband, and when you lose a child you feel like you have let everyone down and you feel like giving up. After going through these trying and depressing times I was able to deliver 3 (not all at the same time of course) healthy babies and they are truly a blessing to me!

My words of encouragement/advice are put God first, be strong, do not give up, and have faith and through it all it will work out for the best.

Lajuana's Story

In November 2002, I found out I was pregnant. It was a planned pregnancy and one that I was very excited about. I had a daughter that I gave birth to in 1998 and never planned on having any more children. Five years later I changed my mind. I remember surprising my family by wrapping baby bottles in Christmas paper for my family to open up at the same time. Months passed, and my pregnancy seemed normal. On March 20, 2003, I woke up to begin my day. While using the bathroom, I heard a loud pop and when I looked, I saw nothing but blood. I rushed to my husband to tell him to take me to the hospital as soon as possible. We got our daughter together and dropped her off to preschool and went to Robert Wood Johnson hospital in Hamilton, NJ.

I had never experienced my water breaking, nor had I experienced bleeding while pregnant so I was quite frantic. While registering, I went to the receptionist and insisted that I be seen because I was bleeding and pregnant. I was taken to the maternity department and was given a hospital room to sit in. At the time, I had no idea what was going on and was quite concerned. The ultra-sonographer came to get me and did an ultrasound. During the ultrasound I asked questions about the baby, but the technician was extremely quiet. My fear developed into terror and I was taken back to my room. The nurses tried to put an IV in, but I was so dehydrated that they had trouble finding a vein. Once they found a vein, I felt the liquid entering my body and became sleepy.

While lying in the bed, I woke up and yelled, "the baby is coming". I began screaming and felt my baby literally slide out of me. I was very hysterical at this time and the nurse told me that the baby was not breathing. When I heard those words, I recall screaming "No!" repeatedly. Once I calmed down, the nurse asked me if I wanted to see the baby and I told them "no". Both my husband and my mother were in the room with me and did view the baby. I was almost 19 weeks pregnant and on that day my world fell apart.

I was sent to the operating room and the doctor's performed a Dilation and Curettage also known as a D & C. While in the recovery room, my husband and I were faced with the worst decision ever. We had to decide to either give my child a funeral or have her cremated. My husband decided that it was best to have her cremated to spare us from the agony of her untimely passing. As I prepared to leave the hospital without my baby, they were generous enough to give us a package that included our baby's footprints and hat. I chose to add my sonogram of her to this package and all the cards and well wishes and placed it securely in my basement. Her name was Bethany Fogg and she was 7.8 oz. and 25 cm.

Three months after giving birth prematurely, I found out that I was pregnant with my son. Of course I was nervous that my third pregnancy would end up like 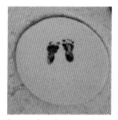 my second pregnancy. The doctor decided to give me a cerclauge to prevent my cervix from opening up too soon. I spent the majority of this pregnancy trying to remain positive. Around my 32nd week, I was eating at a restaurant and went into labor. I immediately went to the hospital where it was confirmed that I was in labor. The doctor gave me medicine to stop the contractions and I was sent home to be on bed rest until my baby was born. The bed rest was successful and my son, who was originally due on the day after his sister passed away, was born on February 29, 2004. Needless to say, we were very happy to welcome our baby boy early but not too early. Prior to having him, I read an article about a woman who experienced the same thing I did and named her son Jaden. Jaden is Hebrew for " thankful". I decided to name my son Jaden and I am extremely thankful to God for giving me another chance at motherhood. Although my experience was one that I would not want anyone to endure, I must say that I have become a stronger person as a result and cherish every day that I have with my children. Jaden will always be a constant reminder of what I have had to endure and what I have overcome.

Donna's Story

My husband and I were married both at age 20, and ready to begin the rest of our lives together. We wanted children right away so we did not wait to try. After many years of no luck getting pregnant on our own, we discussed going to see a specialist in this field. We found one but I was very over weight at the time and he told us that he would not help us because of that. So we put that thought aside for a while until we met a doctor that said he could help us. It was a whirlwind of tests for both of us and lots of time involved. We started with injections and then went to in-vitro.

Along the way we had many miscarriages and disappointments. I was constantly in the office; it felt like I lived there. Blood tests, ultrasounds, etc. There would be a month where there was no news and others of good news that we were finally pregnant, only to lose that pregnancy early on in miscarriage. I think there were a total of 10 miscarriages throughout our entire time of trying.

In May of 1994 we started Metrodin injections that my husband gave to me. My first pregnancy was in June 1994 and the doctors were watching the levels very carefully, my Doctor said that they were worried because my levels were not rising like they should and that I will most likely miscarry. That did happen but we were confident that with one pregnancy there would be others.

48

October 27, 1994, I am pregnant again and in November I lost that one as well. The doctor talked with us about doing a white blood cell transfusion to help from miscarrying.

I was able to get pregnant again in March, 1995 and after doing an ultrasound it came back that we were having twins and our approx. due date would be November 11, 1995. On May 1st we heard their heartbeats, what an awesome time that was. On Wednesday, May 17, 1995 I woke feeling crampy, I called the doctor and they said to take it easy. Around 4 that day my water broke and at 8:15 p.m. I delivered my 1st baby in the toilet, which was stillborn; the ambulance came and took me to the hospital. After examining me, they said that there was a chance that I could carry the 2nd baby but no guarantees. Around 4:40 a.m. the next morning my 2nd baby was stillborn. They brought my 2 boys Adam and Ben in to me and laid them on my chest, we kept them with us for a few hours. They were beautiful babies. Heaven was a sweeter place with them in it. Many people came and supported us at their funeral. God bless all of our family and friends.

On January 11, 1996 the results came back positive and I was pregnant again. All levels were

49

doing well and the baby was strong. In March they stitched my cervix so that I would have a better chance of keeping this pregnancy. On May 11, 1996 I started having problems and they took me into the hospital with plans to keep me on bedrest but my baby girl had other ideas. They unstitched my cervix and out little girl Caitlyn was born. She lived for 4 ½ hours before God took her home. David was able to hold her and then gave her to me and they took me to a room, as we got to the door a baby started crying and they tried to get me in the room and shut the door quickly but it was not quick enough. It is very hard holding your precious baby and knowing she is going to die and then to hear another baby cry, it is indescribable. I would have given anything to hear her cry. We had the funeral for Caitlyn and after I grew stronger we tried again. There were many pregnancies to come after that.

In April 1997 we found out we were pregnant again with twins and all the levels were very good and rising high.   This would be a very high-risk pregnancy and much monitoring by the doctors. In June everything changed. I started bleeding very bad and they admitted me and told me that I had just landed myself in the hospital and on bedrest for a very long time. After several weeks in the hospital I was able to go home on bedrest and my wonderful dad sat with me every day while David was at work, what a great time that was between him and I. We had many ultrasounds and bloods drawn throughout this entire pregnancy there were ups and downs but the doctors kept reassuring me that they felt that I would carry to term. In July 1997 after much prayer and work at keeping these babies safe inside me, they decided that it was going to be their birthday. So on July 17th I delivered my 1st baby stillborn and on the 18th my 2nd baby was stillborn. We named them Daniel and Emma. They almost lost me this time around. They had to rush me into surgery to stop the bleeding which they did, but the doctors told David that they do not want me to get pregnant any more, it is to much on my body and it is not worth the risk of my life. So we agreed with them.

After the funeral David and I had been talking about adoption and we started the process and we now have 2 beautiful children, a girl 15 and a boy 21 months old. What a joy they are to our family. Adoption is the best gift that a birthparent can give to their child if they can't raise them. We have a beautiful family and God is watching over my birth children in heaven till we meet again.

Through all of these pregnancies God was #1 in my life and my husbands. He was the only thing that got us through all of our trials. Many people would ask me how I do it time after time and my only answer would be GOD!

My prayers go out to all of you that are going through hard times right now and I would like you to know that all you have to do is look to God and if you truly know Him as your personal Savior He will guide you through and will hold your hand and put his arms of protection around you. Just lean on Him and He will guide your paths.
God Bless!

What seems so natural is truly a miracle from God
By Rasheida Marie Washington

I always knew I would be a mom. Growing up I had the most nurturing, caring mom a kid could ask for and I wanted to be just like her. I would raise my child/children just the way she did. My kids would be my world. We would do things together so that they were well rounded-family vacations, sports, girl/boy scouts, oh and of course church.

Proverbs 22:6 Train up a child in the way he should go, and when he is old he will not depart from it.

This was what my parents did for me and I was going to do it for mine. As a child I love children. I was always playing with the younger ones. I was the older kid that played with the younger kids. I had my own "school". The kids on my block would gather in my yard every day and I would "teach them". I taught them their A, B, C's, how to tie their shoes and of course, bible verses. So it was just a natural progression for me to have my own.

I imagined how many I would have-one boy and one girl, the perfect family. I had names picked out and everything. So when I got married on February 3, 2003 I knew it was only a matter of time. I became pregnant almost immediately (that honeymoon was something else☺) and the planning began.

Of course I had to find out what I was having. My husband didn't want to know but after finding out I was having a girl, I didn't know how I

was going to contain myself. A little mini me, Wow!!!
I was going to be a mom.

Fast forward to August 7, 2003 a regular day
in my pregnancy or so I thought. After an evening
out and some ice cream to top it off, I began to
have severe chills. When they wouldn't stop after 10
or so minutes I knew something wasn't right. We
called the afterhour's doctor who suggested that I
go to the ER. Once arriving there I was told I was
in labor and they would do all they could to stop it
but needed to transfer me to another hospital
because they didn't have a NICU. Everything
happened so fast and some of the details I believe I
erased from my mind but at 3:00 a.m. on August 8th
Leazar Jahlani Washington was born. She was only
23 weeks, weighed less than a pound, and her lungs
were not developed enough. You have to remember
this was 10 years ago and medicine was not as it is
today. The doctors informed us that she would not
survive so after spending 3 and ½ hours with her we
made the most painful decision I've ever had to
make and took her off of the ventilator. At 3:59
a.m. she went home to be with the Lord.

Leaving that hospital empty handed was so
surreal. If any of you have ever watched a Spike Lee
film where everything around you is moving but you

54

feel like you're standing still?? Well that's how I felt and I will never forget that feeling. Who wants to bury your child?

After the loss I thought I would just get pregnant again and everything would be fine. A year went by and nothing. My husband and I made the decision to go see a specialist. After some testing it was discovered that the previous loss I had caused damaged to my tubes and I was told I'd "never get pregnant on my own". So what did I do? Pray? Nope, **I** decided that wasn't going to happen. I was going to have my child at **ALL** cost. I asked the doctor what she we do next and she suggested IVF. Anyone who knows me knows I do not do needles but again at **ALL** cost: and so it began. Countless doctor's visits, medications, hair growing in places it shouldn't☺ and of course the needles, in the rear nonetheless.

I hated every minute of it and after two unsuccessful rounds of treatment I decided to "get off of this roller coaster ride". Of course the doctor tried to talk me out of it because my insurance would pay for one more round (they were all about the money) but I stood my ground and did what I should've done from the beginning-PRAY.

I began to seek God's word and promises for childbirth. I read every scripture I could find. I also came across a life-changing book called Supernatural Childbirth by Jackie Mize. I read it several times. My husband read it. We highlighted scriptures, wrote confessions in the book and began to believe God. There is a song we used to sing at church (written by Becky Fender), which asks a question? "Whose report shall you believe?" In the next line is echoed, "We shall believe the report of the Lord!" The chorus affirms. This is what my husband and I chose to do.

Six months after starting the IVF treatments and 3 years after losing our first child, Landyn Gabriel Washington was born. **GOD DID IT!!!!!.** Although I would not wish the pain of losing a child on any one, I now know that God is always in control. Through my experience I have been able to support and encourage other women who have similar experiences.

When you learn what your role is as a woman you automatically assume that you will get pregnant and have children but ***What seems so natural is truly a miracle from God.***

Monica's Story
"Embracing the Unexpected"

It was fall of 1978. I was eagerly heading to college of all places "Hotlanta". I had always visited my friend Lynn there in Decatur, Georgia and I had set my sights on that area for college. Not for the academic promise, but because they had the best parties and the cutest boys. Just to give you a little background, I went there to prove to myself and to my parents that I could finish four years of school and earn a degree in Business Administration. I had become interested in business through a course of study in high school called "BOE" (Business and Office Education). I aced typing, and a few others skills that went along with that course. I said certainly this is the field of study for me. I always lacked confidence in learning anything new, so when I excelled in this particular subject, I knew I had found my life's work. However, there was a subject that I had not done so well in, as a matter of fact failed miserably; although spending countless hours talking about it, watching movies, and making myself as ready as possible, and that was the subject of "boys."

I was quite promiscuous as a teenager, I was underdeveloped (in the area of anatomy), I had dental issues, I did not have the "good hair" (all the African American girls of the 60s know what I am referring to) and I just did not know who I was. So that made me very vulnerable, naïve and a target. Moving on to my story, I was off to Atlanta, storage trunk in tow, my red bedspread with matching curtains, popcorn popper and orange 13 inch TV, ready for the world and to live away from home for the first time. Wow, this was going to be great!

My fate was waiting for me before I arrived, because I was told that a young man who was related by marriage to one of my family members lived there. "You should meet up with him", I was told. Okay yes, my good time was already waiting for me...fresh meat; of course I did not know the prey would be me. I forged ahead making the contact after settling in the dorm, and reconnecting with an old classmate from my hometown. I also had met my roommate by now, and we clicked as friends, but did not hang out together, she was there for school, so we did not have anything in common along those lines.

Fast-forwarding, I connected with the young man and we begin to see each other (and I do not mean with just the eyes), REALLY see each other almost immediately. I found myself spending the night at his home in Decatur and catching the bus to school (oh by the way, he was not in school, he owned his own business and about 5 years my senior). Shortly thereafter (around October) I begin to feel sick, tired all the time and just not feeling myself. My roommate encouraged me to go and see the nurse in which I did. She informed me that I was pregnant; she might as well I have told me that I had a terminal disease. I was devastated to say the least. What would my parents say? I was about to give them the biggest disappointment of all, I would not finish college, they would not be proud of me. The biggest let down of all, I would not know if I would have completed college. My immediate thought was to have an abortion, which would fix everything. I just could not face my mom with this news. My future was laid out; my parents were prepared to pay cash for my education (back then it was about $3,500 a year...WOW). After talking with a family member, who encouraged me not to go through with the abortion; I decided to keep the baby and face my parents. I will skip the details of the conversation; it is a little murky anyway.

Shortly after making the decision to keep the baby, I also fabricated the "big lie" and said that we had gotten married, that way it would not be as bad. Well, I was so wrong. This man turned out to be Dracula, Frankenstein, Dr. Jekyll and Mr. Hyde. He began to physically abuse me on a regular basis, seemingly looking for reasons to strike me. House not clean, chrome not shined whatever. I was strangled, slapped, gun drawn on me among the worst. I was stressed, always fearful, crying and feeling very alone. I had left my parents' home and care and was now at the mercy of a monster. I had nowhere to go, no one to turn to...I thought.

We went home to visit on a particular weekend (by now I am five months pregnant) I had become extremely excited about being a mom, and had picked out a name for a boy "Jeremy." One night in particular, there was some type of disagreement, I had begun to spot by this time and I was resting in bed. My mother was very graciously tending to all my needs. "Jack" (not his real name) and I were having a "discussion" in the bedroom which was somewhat heated on his part and my mom knew something was wrong. Long story short, he was asked to leave that night. I begin to hemorrhage very badly and the ambulance was called. I was rushed to the ER, and all I remember was a grim look on the Dr.'s face and immediately I felt the baby pass through my womb. I must have passed out, because I do not remember anything else except waking up in recovery. Again, I was devastated. After a period of resting and getting my health back, I returned to Georgia but not the same. My thoughts were totally consumed with the loss of my baby.

Every TV commercial that I saw, every new mother or pregnant woman brought me grief. I used to stare at the maternity clothes that I wore. I just could not believe this had happened to me. Needless to say, the relationship with the "Dr." ended and I returned to my hometown, although I was not separated from those thoughts of loss. I remember attending a baby shower for my best girlfriend and I could not endure everyone else's jubilation. I retreated to a nearby bedroom and begin to weep. To me it felt as if the world stood still.

In July of 1980, a young man witnessed to me about being Born Again and accepting Jesus Christ as my personal Lord and Savior. I eagerly accepted that invitation and I knew in that moment that I was made whole emotionally and mentally. It was a brand new start; all of the surface things that caused me depression, hopelessness and despair had left my life. I say surface because the loss of my child and a failed relationship I knew hurt, but there are so many things buried deep in our soul, that we just push pass and they are never dealt with. That's another topic on another day.

Shortly, thereafter I married the man who led me to the Lord and I of course immediately wanted to have children. We married December 5th of 1980 and I gave birth to a baby girl, September 23rd 1981. Her name is Tamar Knibye; yes the author of this book. Little did I know that she would experience the same loss, but instead use her pain to reach out to others and give them hope. You can begin again; you can be a parent and pour your life into the life of a child through love, nurturing and care. Be it through natural birth or adoption. In the years to come we had two more children and adopted a beautiful baby boy. I encourage you to not suppress your pain, but confront it head on. Talk to someone, or better still, ask Jesus Christ into your heart. He makes all things beautiful...in His time. To God Be the Glory.

Each story, though different, had something in common. Every woman noted here and throughout society had to heal from the loss. You have taken the first step to your healing by picking up this book and I congratulate you as a woman, a strong woman. But sometimes it takes more than just talking about it. There are specific steps that need to be taken to begin the healing process. To find out more and to continue healing pick up our brief continuation of "Letting Go of Baby" called "What's Next? – A guide to dealing with grief after a loss".

To contact us we can be emailed at
Tamarknibye@groups.facebook.com.
To access our website go to
www.facebook.com/groups/Tamarknibye.

Kadesh (left front), Tamar (left back), Tsombawi III (front right), and Tsombawi Jr. (right back)

Printed in Great Britain
by Amazon